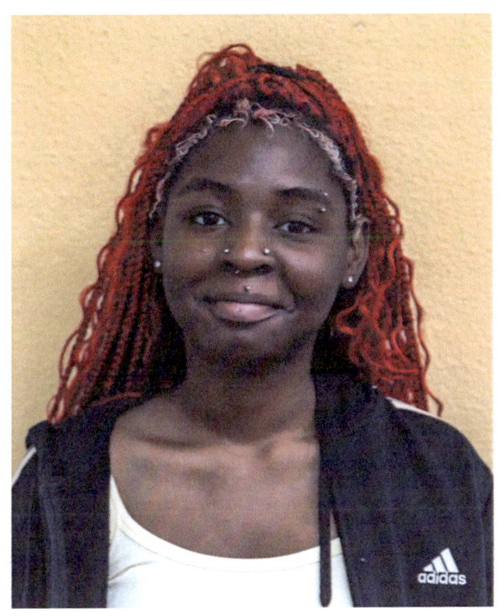

B R I A N N A   E D L E R

My Dad Died

This story reminds me of my dad and the good memories I had with him. It reminds me to appreciate my time with loved ones, because they could leave at any time.

66

Eventually everyone has to go
and you will never know when or how.
Embrace the happy memories, embrace the bad
ones too because one day those might
be all you have.

When my dad died, I didn't know how to properly feel my emotions at all. I don't think I even cried. It took me a while to actually process that he was gone. The fondest memory I have of him is when we're out picking pecans from a tree together, a memory that makes me smile and feel close to him. The grassy smell tickling my nose and the strong winds gave me a chill.

His passing really shocked me at the time. I was only 12 years old, and having a parent die never crossed my mind that it would happen to me. I always thought that he would either live forever or at least live a long life at least until he was like 100. It made me realize that no matter what or how hard you try, eventually everyone has to die no matter how close you are.

For some reason I couldn't get myself to cry even though I wanted to really bad. I was sad but I couldn't even shed a single tear. That made me feel as if I was weird. I tried to force myself by listening to sad music, that kinda worked. Eventually though, I finally did cry and when I did I couldn't stop. I'm usually not a cryer at all, most of the time I keep my emotions bottled up and my feelings to myself. Even though I rarely did see my father, I did still love him unconditionally. Regardless if my family liked him or not for his past actions, I still loved him with my whole heart. Speaking of his alleged past actions, according to my uncle he had walked in on my dad doing something very inappropriate with me. Personally, I don't and probably won't ever believe that my father could ever do something like that to me. But obviously I wouldn't know, because I was a baby and my uncle is dead now.

Even so, my father was still good and tried his best to be there, rumors or not. But it wasn't all sunshine and rainbows the whole time he was alive. One of the saddest memories I had with him was when I had asked him to attend a father daughter muffin day at my elementary school, as expected he didn't show up. I wasn't very surprised though it wasn't his first time pulling a stunt like this.

He would always say and promise me that he would come but when the time came. He would have an excuse like how he didn't have a ride, that he had to work or sometimes not even answer the phone. Eventually though I got used to it and got used to not feeling sad or holding a grudge against him. Over the years though I started to understand why he couldn't make it and realized he was telling the truth and all the excuses he had weren't fake.

My father may have not been the best in other people's eyes, but to me he was the most best and precious thing to me. Those memories that we had together I will forever cherish and adore them forever until the day I die.

This experience made me realize that you really do need to appreciate the time you have with a loved one. Eventually everyone has to go and you will never know when or how. Embrace the happy memories, embrace the bad ones too because one day those might be all you have.

A Moment That Changed Me

I want people to know what I went through,
that they are not alone, and that they are
strong.

66

I almost died from septic shock. I was always an active girl. I joined a club called Junior ROTC and I made friends who became like family. That club made me start to go on runs, and I also started to paint. Eventually I also picked up on reading. My grades also got better. Life felt like I was going on the right path, but there were some detours along the way.

It felt good knowing what I was doing with my life. But even then, I still made some mistakes and they were not great and now I see that they were wrong. One day, I shared an inappropriate photo on my Instagram story that caused me to get in trouble. My mom asked me why I did it, and I told her that I was looking for attention. I learned that just because I want someone's love or attention, doesn't mean that I need to get it in that way. Thankfully, I learned from my mistakes. But there was always something trying to creep in my life.

School was great. It was a way for me to not be home, where

things didn't always feel safe. I didn't like being home because there was always someone trying to start a fight. My mom always came home tired. The house always felt depressing or too quiet. Being in that club was a safe place for me. It filled me with joy, a warm feeling, like having friends who feel like family. They made me comfortable every time I went to afterschool practice.

One day everything changed for me. I got sick out of nowhere. Every time I ate something, I would vomit everything. I had a very high fever. I couldn't stand up for longer than a minute. I felt like my vision was getting blurry. My head was dizzy and I would smell sickness or the bad smell of pills. I couldn't even lay down or sit. I was just in the bathroom vomiting. My mom took me to the hospital but they told her nothing was wrong with me. I was upset because I knew that something was wrong but they just sent me home. I was still in the bathroom vomiting, crying to my mom, telling her that I couldn't handle it. My mom took me to the hospital again but this time it was serious. I fell unconscious. There were moments when I knew what was going on but it wasn't clear. All I remember was the ambulance telling me that they were taking me to a different hospital because this one was only for adults. They couldn't help me there, so they had to move me. After that, I didn't know what happened. I lost consciousness again. The last thing I remember was seeing my mom's devastated face.

The doctor told my mom that there was a 65% chance that I would make it out alive. They said it would be a miracle if I lived, because the sepsis infected my bloodstream and my lungs. My organs were shutting down. The doctors tried to keep my heart and brain alive. My body was swollen and they said it was possible that I would lose some limbs, like my wrists and feet. I did lose some of my fingertips and it did leave me with some scars, but my body proved them wrong. I survived. Even though I lost my old life, there are different ways to look at life and from a different perspective. I appreciate being given another opportunity to make things better.

Life can be a struggle but you can push through it. Sometimes people will bring you down and give you bad looks, but those are only temporary moments. There are times when I break down, but I learn to get back up and live a positive happy life, and sometimes joke around about my situation to brighten people's day. For those who are going through something like this, you're not the only one. I'm here with you.

A N T O N I O   G A N D Y   I V

A Place to Call Home

I want people to understand my struggle and I
hope that people can relate to me.

*Since we've been here,
I've made a lot of friends and I love it
here now. I am humbled because there are people
in the world who are less fortunate than us.*

Growing up I didn't really have stable housing, but my parents always put in the effort to make sure that we had a place to live. Whether we slept at our uncles, aunts, or cousin's house for the night, we still had a place to sleep. We moved to California for a better lifestyle. We stayed at our aunt's house for a while, and fast forward to 2019 we got our first apartment. We were so excited. My mom started to make a lot of money working with elderly people. We bought a playstation, X Box and Nintendo. Our school McAuliffe Elementary School also blessed us with money to get settled in our new house. My mom cried with joy and appreciation. She used the money to buy us a TV. Everything was going good until Covid 19 hit.

Our neighbors had a water leak that got into our house and destroyed everything. The landlord was supposed to pay for everything during the pandemic, but instead, she started to avoid us and we ended up being evicted. We went to stay with our auntie again, but eventually she ended up getting orders to move to Maryland. We really wanted to go with her, but she couldn't let us go. We were upset that we couldn't go and became homeless.

We ended up moving to a shelter. My dad moved into a men's shelter, and we stayed in a different shelter with our mom for two years. When our time was up, the director of the shelter took us to the airport because my mom thought it would be safer to stay there instead of on the streets. We stayed there for one week. My mom ended up getting hurt so we had to push her around in a wheelchair. Two of the security guards at the airport bought us food so we wouldn't be hungry. We were very appreciative.

My dad wanted to come get us but his shelter wouldn't allow it, which made him very upset. He thought about leaving the shelter but my mom talked him out of it. Two days later he came to get us. When we left the airport, we caught the trolley to Carlsbad where we used to live and stayed at a Motel 6. My dad came the next day and we bounced back and forth at hotels together. One hotel was nice, they provided breakfast for us, but it would cost my dad a thousand dollars for us to continue staying there. My dad's money started to get low so he picked up extra hours at his job at Ikea. During that time, we were trying to go to shelters to see if we could get in. Some didn't allow us to enter because there were pedophiles there. My mom was sad and lost all hope. At some point it got easy, but we started accumulating more clothes and it was hard to bring everything along with us.

I heard my parents talking about the money getting low and it made me scared of being homeless and staying on the street. I heard a lot of bad stories about people staying on the streets. We ended up on the waitlist at Father Joe's Villages. They gave us a six month timeframe, but my mom ended up calling every week for a year straight. When we finally got accepted, I was upset because I didn't like the outside of the building. It smelled horrible, and there were a lot of homeless people around. I was scared because I would have to wake up at 5am to catch the trolley to make it to school in Clairemont. But it ended up working out. We even met a new cousin that ended up staying at the shelter with us. Since we've been here, I've made a lot of friends and I love it here now. I am humbled because there are people in the world who are less fortunate than us. I get to have a roof over my head, surrounded by people who love me, while others are still on the streets.

G E N A R O   Z A M O R A

Drawing War Scenarios Saved Me

This shows me that I can get away from my problems. I learned something I like. Drawing war scenarios helped me.

66

I like to draw war scenarios to help poor people.

When I lived in Texas my life was very hard. My mom had an abusive boyfriend and there was a lot of screaming and sadness. I was scared for me but for my mom and my sister too. I remember hiding in my room and feeling scared but also feeling like I wanted to punch a wall. I couldn't do it. I didn't want my mom to worry about me. I always had trouble writing and expressing myself which made it harder for me to feel better.

One day, I had to write at school and I was nervous. It is hard for me to focus and concentrate and sometimes letters switch places. I felt like I wanted to do it but I was upset that it seemed so hard. I started drawing instead. I started drawing war scenarios. I don't know why but it made me feel good. It made me feel like I could picture something and put it on paper. It made sense and a lot didn't make sense in my life.

Some people think it's a little weird that I like to draw war scenarios but I think that it's organized and I can control what I draw. I am good at drawing and that makes me feel like I'm good at something. One of my favorite war scenarios to draw is a big wasteland. There are three rich people and they rule the world with their greed. The poor people have had enough of their bad treatment so they get together to start a revolution. They fight and fight with all that they have but in all my scenarios my mind draws the poor people losing. This makes me feel more depressed. I don't give up and I keep drawing them. I know that one day they will win. Drawing specifically war scenarios helps me when things in my life feel too hard to handle. My mom, my sister and I left her abusive boyfriend and fled to San Diego. That is how we ended up at Father Joe's Villages. Here, I feel safer and I can keep drawing my war scenarios. When I was stressed I realized that drawing war scenarios would help me a lot. I felt a little less angry and a little more strong. Today, I still have some trouble with school and learning but I know that I still have something that is mine and that I am good at.

I want to finish school and join the military some day. I want to use the war scenarios in my head to help the poor people fight the greedy rich people and people who hurt others. I will use my creative mind and maybe get to be captain and lead a real army some day. I also plan to create a military coloring book for scared kids like me. It is my super power and I can use it to keep me, my sister, my mom safe and others safe.

After Pin Pon

This is meaningful for me because my cousin
died and I now have my dog. I was depressed
but my dog makes me happy.

“

My cousin Pin Pon had been
kidnapped by the Mexican cartel in Sinaloa,
Mexico. This was one of the biggest reasons why I
felt very sad and depressed.

It was a normal day, I was 14 years old, when I got news that made my heart stop. My mom's eyes were popping out of her head and her hands were shaking. I had just gotten home from school and I knew something bad had happened. My cousin Pin Pon had been kidnapped by the Mexican cartel in Sinaloa, Mexico. He was missing for 3 days and he was found brutally beaten, and was missing his eyes. A stranger found his dead body under a pile of tires and leaves. It was horrible. I can still feel the terror in my mom's eyes. This was one of the biggest reasons why I felt very sad and depressed. One thing that helped me with the depression was my dog Niño.

They didn't want to tell me that they had found his dead body. I knew they had news when I got out of school but they did not want to tell me. I was in school at Monarch School near Father Joe's Villages. I had to get to Tijuana, so I walked to the trolley with my brother and went to Mexico to be with my family. I was shaking the whole way. My brother was quiet the whole time. He asked me what had happened, but I told him that my mom had said to wait and not say anything. He knew something was wrong and he just stayed quiet. When we got to Tijuana, my mom confirmed it in the car. It was my mom, my mom's ex-girlfriend, my 3 cousins and my brother.

After that, I felt very sad and didn't want to do much. I felt like I couldn't feel my emotions. I didn't know what to say to anyone. I couldn't make him come back to life. I remember my brother having nightmares. He could hear the screams and he even said he had seen what happened to Pin Pon in his dreams before it happened. One day my mom's ex-girlfriend came home with a surprise to cheer me up. It was night time in March, two years ago, not too long after the terrible incident with Pin Pon. She said it would help me feel happiness again. The surprise was a little puppy. He was a perfect little black ball of fur with a white chest. It was love at first sight. I named him Niño. He was a late birthday surprise.

Niño makes me happy. He reminds me that there is good in the world. Niño sleeps with me in my bed, when he wants to, and he makes me feel loved and safe. I named him Niño because he is just like a little kid. He's my kid. Although I will always miss my cousin Pin Pon and all the memories that we had together, having Niño has really filled a big hole that had been left in my heart. I feel happier at home and at school. I know that I will always have love and I will be okay.

ANTONIO GANDY V

My Voice Matters

It's important to share my story and show how
bullying affects people.

I realized that not everyone
is nice and not everyone is meant to be your friend.
But some people can be trusted. Now, knowing
that, I am at peace with everything that
happened in fourth grade.

Life was good at Stuart Mesa elementary school. I had lots of friends. My best friend's name was Jayana. We lived on Camp Pendleton. They had their own school on base. After school, we used to hang out, and my friends would go to the store every day. Then, every Friday, we would buy cookies, ice cream, and juice from the school. Then we would explore the sewers, crawling through them, and we also loved exploring the desert. We played football and rode our bikes all around the neighborhood.

Then everything changed. My auntie went back to Maryland and we could not come with her, so we moved into a shelter. I had to change schools to Breezehill Elementary School. When I was in the fourth grade, I was on the chubby side. I was bigger than most fourth graders, so that's what they used to make fun of me about. They used to call me names, like "fat ass." Even when I didn't do anything, they would still bully me. I would tell the principal, but all she would do was tell them to stop. They would know I had told, and they would keep doing it. I used to come home sad and tell my mom. She would call the school, but they would lie to her, acting like they were handling it. Then I would go back to school, and they would call me a snitch and start hitting me. I would tell the staff, but they would ignore my complaints and do nothing about it.

The year ended, and I went to fifth grade. The day I stood up for myself, I was in science class. I was sitting next to my friend, and we were doing our work when this kid started talking about us. We were trying to ignore him, but he was getting louder. Then he left the class because the teacher called him to the office. He was gone for like three minutes, then he came back to the class looking mad.

I looked at him, and he said, "What the fuck are you looking at?" I told him no one cares if he's mad. Then he got in my face. I said, "You're not going to do anything," but before I had a chance to back up, he smacked me on the face. I pushed him back, then he ran up on me. I punched him in the jaw, then he hit me back. He grabbed a metal rod to throw at me, but he missed. Then he grabbed a chair and threw it at me. I moved out of the way, and it almost hit these two kids.

I backed him up into the cabinet, and we started fighting. Then the teachers pulled me off him. We both got sent to the principal's office and were suspended for one day. When I came back, I got kicked out of making a car group, but most of the fifth graders were happy I stood up for myself. He and I ended up going on a field trip together.

But now, since I got bullied, it changed how I see everyone as my friend. I realized that not everyone is nice and not everyone is meant to be your friend. But some people can be trusted. Now, knowing that, I am at peace with everything that happened in fourth grade.

Special Thanks to Our Sponsors

The Wright Voice Award program would not be possible without the generous support of our sponsors and community partners.

We extend our heartfelt gratitude to Father Joe's Villages in San Diego for partnering with us to bring The Wright Voice Award January 2026 program to life and for supporting the courage, creativity, and growth of the young storytellers featured in this collection.

We would also like to give special recognition to our Gold Sponsors for their generous support:

Isaac Wright

Brian Marsh

Susan Perkins

Because of your support, these young writers were given the opportunity to discover the power of their voice, share their stories, and be celebrated for their creativity and bravery.

Your investment in youth and storytelling helps ensure that every voice has the chance to be heard.

With sincere appreciation,
The Wright Press

9 798234 032225